KNOWLEDGE ENCYCLOPEDIA
ANCIENT
CIVILISATIONS
INVENTIONS & DISCOVERIES

Wonder House

(An imprint of Prakash Books)

contact@wonderhousebooks.com

ISBN : 9789390391356

Table of Contents

ARMS AND THE MAN

Human beings did not always walk on two feet. Our early ancestors walked on all fours. **Fossils** and other discoveries made by archaeologists show that our ape-like forefathers only began to walk upright between six- and three-million years ago. Once their arms were free, they were able to learn and do things that had never before been possible.

With the free use of arms, early human beings became smarter at handling things. Their creativity, combined with a natural curiosity, opened up a brave new world of inventions and discoveries for them! So what were their greatest finds? Who were the brightest inventors? Read on to discover more about the inventions of ancient civilisations.

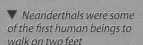
▼ *Neanderthals were some of the first human beings to walk on two feet*

Material Progress

Look at any timeline of human history and you will notice that historians track human progress in terms of when certain materials were invented and used. Glass, paper, mortar, metals, and cloth are all a part of this timeline. Some materials are so important to us that historical periods have been named after them. The Stone Age, the Bronze Age and the Iron Age are classified according to when stone, bronze, and iron were used to create tools and technologies.

⊙ Incredible Individuals

Over 3 million years ago, the ancestors of humans began making stone tools. Among these early inventors was East Africa's *Australopithecus afarensis*. The most popular member of this species is Lucy. She was discovered by Donald Johanson and Tom Gray in 1974 in Hadar, Ethiopia. While Lucy was not the first to be discovered, her discovery revolutionised our understanding of human evolution; most importantly, that our brain size increased after we became **bipedal**

◀ *Bone fragments of Lucy, who lived some 3.2 million years ago*

2.58 MILLION YEARS AGO

This marked the start of the Palaeolithic Period, or the Old Stone Age. However, the world's earliest stone tools were even older. They belonged to **proto humans** who lived 3.3 million years ago, near Lake Turkana in East Africa.

C. 1.5 MILLION YEARS AGO

Evidence shows that humans used fire for light, warmth, and to keep insects and predators away.

600,000 YEARS AGO

The earliest known man-made hearth or fireplace lay inside the Qesem Cave in Israel. About 15–20 people may have lived there and used fire for cooking.
In fact, cooking food regularly may have played a role in expanding the brain!

500,000 YEARS AGO

In England, a Stone Age horse was discovered with a hole in its shoulder bone, made by a wooden spear.

The oldest stone-tipped spears were seen in South Africa.

c. 170,000 YEARS AGO

Humans began covering their bodies with clothes at this point. The first lice belong to the same time. Do you think there is a connection between the invention of clothes and the evolution of lice?

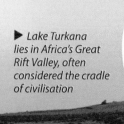

▶ *Lake Turkana lies in Africa's Great Rift Valley, often considered the cradle of civilisation*

Ethiopia

Lake Turkana

Kenya

▶ *Australopithecus afarensis looked part-ape and part-human*

Breakthroughs by Early Humans

Learning human history is not easy. Time, climate, and changing circumstances have destroyed many ancient artefacts. The Stone Age is regarded as the period in history when—across the world—early human tribes were using tools of wood, bone, and stone. Over time, humans have used many types of amazing materials to invent complex structures that made their lives comfortable, efficient, and sophisticated.

In Real Life

Do you imagine that only humans hunted animals with spears? Then you will be amazed by the videos of a group of chimpanzees in Africa that use spears to hunt galagos. Researchers have been able to spot the chimps hunting them about 22 times!

▶ *Galagos, also called bush babies, are smaller primates hunted by these chimps*

c. 26,000 BCE

Clay was used to make figurines, such as the Venus of Dolni Vestonice. She even bore the fingerprints of an ancient human child who held her!

18,000 BCE

Clay vessels were made by early humans. Some of the oldest clay pots were found in Xianrendong Cave in China.

c. 6000 BCE

Bricks were used to make the world's first cities. The ruins at Jericho, Turkey, belong to the oldest known city in our knowledge.

5550–5000 BCE

Ancient Egyptians invented linen cloth, spindles, and looms. Ancient Indians discovered the uses of cotton. Metal daggers were created.

◀ *The Venus of Dolni Vestonice, the oldest known clay figurine*

◀ *Sun-dried bricks were made in Ur, an ancient city in Mesopotamia in c. 4000 BCE*

All That Glitters

The Copper Age, also called the Chalcolithic Age, began 9000–11,000 years ago. It is dated from around 4000–2000 BCE. It was the first time that humans began using metals. Early humans found that by heating copper, you could make it less hard and more malleable. This meant that they could beat it, melt it, mould it, and even mix it with other metals to make it stronger. Copper was easily mined and more durable than stone-made objects. Experimentation with copper led to the first metalwork technologies and the first smiths in the world.

▲ *A bell beaker from Central Europe dating back to the Copper Age*

▲ *Copper in its natural form*

The Bronze Rush

The Copper Age melts into the Bronze Age around 3000 BCE. The Bronze Age began in Greece and China with the discovery of **alloys**. As different cultures learned the science of melting metals together, so the age spread across the globe. For instance, the Bronze Age in some parts of Africa began as late as the 1st millennium BCE.

Bronze is a yellowish alloy of copper and tin. It was used to make weapons, vessels, jewellery, statues, and heaps of other things. As demand for bronze grew, people looked far and wide for new sources of tin, leading to various explorations!

In Real Life

It is generally agreed that gold was the first metal to be discovered by humans. But it turned out to be too soft, too rare, and too expensive for practical daily use. Soon, the knowledge and skill of purifying and fashioning gold also became greatly valued. This is especially seen in ancient Egypt. Discovered in 1922, the tomb of the late Bronze Age pharaoh **Tutankhamun** is a hoard of golden treasures. His expressive funeral mask in particular is an example of the Egyptians' unparalleled craftsmanship.

Necklaces, plates, and rings from a Bronze Age hoard in Denmark

Bronze Age Leaps

After the invention of the wheel and the sailing ship, the first chariots appeared. Trading began, as metals were exchanged for wines and oils. Mathematics became more complex, leading to breakthroughs in astronomy and to improved weights and measures. People could now build spectacular structures like pyramids, temples, and ziggurats. Knowledge poured in from far-off regions. This included different ways of cooking and preserving foods.

▲ Gold bull-headed bracelet from Bronze Age Transylvania

▲ A carving of a Sumerian war chariot

▲ An iron dagger from Anatolia, possibly the first country ever to use iron weapons beginning from around 2000 BCE

▶ Bronze and Iron Age weapons from Romania

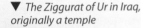

▼ The Ziggurat of Ur in Iraq, originally a temple

Iron Man

Over 1200–300 BCE, iron replaced bronze as the metal of choice. Around 900 BCE, the Egyptians were the first to alloy iron with carbon to create the much lighter and stronger steel. Iron and steel weapons gave civilisations in Greece and Rome a huge advantage. This caused large-scale wars and migrations. Several kingdoms rose and faded during the Iron Age.

▶ The secret of smelting iron ore to fashion tools was a technological breakthrough of the Hittite people of Anatolia

Istanbul
Black Sea
ANATOLIA (MODERN TURKEY)
Pontus
Phrygia
Hatti
Urartu
Cappadocia
Lydia
Hurri
Caria
Mitanni
Lycia
Iraq
Mediterranean Sea
Syria

Exploration and Invention

The Bronze Age saw an explosion of action across the globe. This was largely inspired by the need for metals such as tin, which was needed to make bronze. In the process, people travelled to and explored faraway lands. As they travelled, new trade routes were established. In addition, the means for journeying abroad were created, with inventions such as the wheel and the sailboat. As knowledge passed between cultures, human civilisation profited and progressed.

◀ *An ancient sailboat on the wall of the Temple of Edfu in Egypt*

◀ *The Sun Chariot (c. 1400 BCE) shows the Bronze Age belief that a divine horse pulled the Sun along its path for eternity*

The wheel, later used for pottery and for transport; early sailboats; the gnomon—an early form of the sundial; and the first writing system are invented. The oldest engineered roadway—the Sweet Track—is built using wood in England.

Earliest evidence of man-made glass is seen in **Mesopotamia** and Egypt.

The spoked-wheel and chariot are invented.

The Nebra Sky Disc is the earliest known map of the sky. It is made of bronze and gold. The disc served as a reminder to insert a leap month and has been traced back to Central Europe.

| **c. 4000–3000 BCE** | **c. 3500 BCE** | **2200–1550 BCE** | **c. 1600 BCE** |

👤✓ In Real Life

Glass is made of a material called silicon, which lends its name to the age in which we live. The Silicon Age is dependent on electronic devices such as computers, TVs, cell phones, smart appliances, and so forth. These inventions are powered by silicon chips.

◀ *A Greek amphora (c. 550 BCE) showing a pair of horses harnessed to a chariot with spoked wheels*

Breakthroughs of the Bronze Age

As trade and knowledge grew, record-keeping became necessary. Thus, scripts were invented in the Bronze Age. Cuneiform, the earliest known form of writing, developed in ancient Sumeria. It was considered a gift from the god Enlil. The Chinese developed their script around 1600–1046 BCE by throwing oracle bones. The cracks in the bones were considered the word of god and set down by writers.

▲ The world's oldest coin, the Lydian Lion, is made of electrum, a mix of gold and silver. The Lydians may have been the first people to use gold and silver coins

The first paved trackway called diolkos is built in ancient Greece. It is a line of grooved paving stones connecting two seaports. Goods 'trains' are hauled across it to save shipping costs. Light warships are also transported over the diolkos.

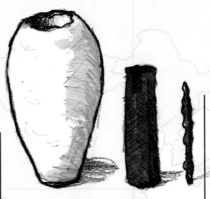

The first battery is made by Parthians in an area that lies in present-day Baghdad. It is made of clay jars filled with vinegar.
Inside each jar is a copper cylinder with an iron rod on top. This early type of battery is most likely used to electroplate silver, which stops it from going black.

Cai Lun invents paper.

600 BCE   **500–400 BCE**   **250 BCE**   **105 BCE**

◀ The Nebra Sky Disc shows the Sun, Moon, and the Pleiades constellation of stars

▶ An old gnomon—the projecting piece on a sundial—from the 7th century Sui dynasty in China

Iron Age Inventors

The creators of the Iron Age lived so long ago, it is no surprise we know little about them. What we do know comes mostly through legends—stories that may or may not be true.

🔍 Archimedes of Syracuse (c. 287–212 BCE)

The story goes that King Hieron II of Syracuse had a goldsmith make him a crown of pure gold. The king suspected, however, that the goldsmith mixed some silver into the crown. King Hieron commanded Archimedes to discover the truth. Though baffled at first, Archimedes found inspiration while taking a bath. As he sank into the bathtub, he saw his body displace a certain volume of water. He realised that you could identify pure metals based on how much water they displaced. He developed this observation into a mathematical concept called the Archimedes's Principle.

▲ A bust of Archimedes of Syracuse

Archimedes made several more contributions to mathematics. He invented a device for raising water called the Archimedes Screw. This is still used in many countries today. He was also a gifted engineer who built the defence and war machines of Syracuse. Tragically, he was killed by Roman soldiers when the army of general Marcus Claudius Marcellus sacked the city.

▶ The Claw of Archimedes was a war machine meant to destroy enemy ships from the city's walls

🔍 Cai Lun of China (c. 62–121 CE)

At the time, Chinese people used silk or bamboo pieces to write upon. Silk was expensive and bamboo was heavy. Cai Lun, an official of the imperial palace, used mashed up bark, hemp, rags, and fishing net to create paper, which was a new writing surface. His assistant Zu Bo improved the quality of paper and soon its popularity spread across the world.

Despite his brilliance, Cai Lun became involved in court politics and fell out of favour with the emperor. When summoned to a public trial, he took a bath, dressed in his finest clothes, and then ended his life by drinking poison.

▲ The ancient Chinese process of papermaking, as outlined by Cai Lun

Hero of Alexandria (lived c. 62 CE)

Hero, or Heron, was a mathematician and engineer of Egypt, then a part of the Roman Empire. He left behind many books on math, mechanics, and logic that are still studied today. Hero enjoyed inventing mechanical novelties such as singing birds and puppets that showcased his theories. He built a fire engine, a water-powered organ, the first syringe, and the first coin-operated machine. He even created a fountain that ran on a type of electricity.

Hero's most famous invention is the aeolipile, the world's first steam engine. However, no one understood its importance at the time. It took civilisation almost 2000 years to rediscover and use the steam engine to make automated machines and vehicles.

▲ *Although most descriptions and ideas of Heron's work were lost, some of them are still kept in Arabic manuscripts*

▲ *A 16th-century model of the aeolipile*

Hero's Aeolipile

Hero's aeolipile was a steam turbine described in his book *Pneumatica*. It was a hollow sphere mounted on a pair of hollow tubes in a way that it was able to turn when steam was let into the sphere through the hollow tubes from a cauldron. Near its middle, the aeolipile had bent tubes that let steam escape and allowed the sphere to revolve in place.

Isn't It Amazing!

In order to recognise and appreciate the contributions of Cai Lun and Archimedes, the modern scientific world named two craters on the Moon in their honour.

◀ *The Archimedes Screw is a device that raises water when a lever is turned. It is still used in some countries, especially for irrigation*

Iron Age Leaders and Thinkers

Apart from inventors, the Iron Age also saw the rise of many deep thinkers and leaders. These people are known today for their contributions to law, philosophy, governance, and abstract science.

▼ *The School of Athens, a fresco at the Vatican, represents philosophy. It depicts some of the most celebrated minds of ancient and medieval times, including Aristotle, Plato, the amazing Hypatia, Ibn-Rushd, Zoroaster, and Alexander the Great. The pioneering mathematicians Euclid, Pythagoras, and Archimedes are also shown. Socrates, Epicurus, Zeno, and Diogenes, each of whom founded a new branch of philosophy, are some other famous figures in this painting*

Chanakya (c. 350–275 BCE)

Chanakya was a teacher and political genius in ancient India. Frustrated with corruption in his country, Chanakya put forth his own ideas and methods for an ideal government. His clever ideas helped his disciple Chandragupta become emperor and establish the powerful Mauryan dynasty.

Chanakya also defeated the army of Alexander the Great at Gandhara—in modern Afghanistan—and forced them to turn back. He put down his great knowledge in the *Arthashastra*, a pioneering book on diplomacy, war, law, taxes, prison, coinage, industry, trade, administration, spies, and other topics. It is mainly owing to Chanakya that the Mauryan empire—from Chandragupta to Emperor Ashoka—became a model of efficient governance.

▲ *Coins of the Mauryan empire*

▲ *A fragment of the Arthashastra*

Euclid (born c. 300 BCE)

Very little is known about the Greek mathematician Euclid, though he left behind some amazing mathematical work in his treatise, *Elements*. Euclid lived and taught in Alexandria, Egypt, during the reign of Ptolemy I Soter during 323–285 BCE. His treatise has continuously impacted human life since the time it was written. Except for the *Bible*, it is perhaps the most translated, published, and studied book in the Western world. Euclid's treatise was the main source of geometric knowledge and reasoning until non-Euclidean geometry came up 2000 years later!

▲ *Euclid's name was derived from the Greek word which means 'Good Glory'*

Sammu-ramat (9th century BCE)

The legendary Sammu-ramat or Semiramis is the first known woman to rule an empire. She came to the throne in 811 BCE upon the death of her husband Shamshi-Adad V. At the time, **Assyria** was poor and weak owing to the late king's mismanagement. Queen Sammu-ramat took the reins of the kingdom and brought stability back to Assyria. Among her many great achievements was the building of the city Babylon, by the River Euphrates. Sammu-ramat led armies to put down uprisings in Persia and Africa, and even to invade India. So heroically did she fight and rule that the inscriptions of the time place her on par with male rulers. In the years after her death, legends claimed her to be the daughter of a goddess!

▲ *Sammu-ramat fighting a lion*

⊛ Incredible Individuals

In 811 BCE, the Neo-Assyrian Empire had the largest territory in the world. It stretched in a bulging triangle between the Mediterranean Sea, Black Sea and Persian Gulf. Egypt and parts of Arabia and North Africa were also a part of this vast empire. When a civil war overtook its royal family, Queen Sammu-ramat rose to power.

Blocks of Civilisation

Around 4,000 BCE, the Sumerians were the first civilisation to build cities across their land. With names like Kish, Lagash, Umma, Eridu, and Uruk, these urban centres had temples, schools, and the tallest buildings ever seen. Like modern cities, they employed huge numbers of people, including carpenters, butchers, smiths, **scribes**, priests, bricklayers, brewers, potters, weavers, jewellers, and even hairdressers. As with other forms of human progress, cities would have been impossible without the invention of certain material technologies.

🔍 Moulding the Earth

Clay is one of the earliest materials exploited by humans. Different communities invented their own methods of using clay to advance civilisation. As a result, the remains of unique styles of earthenware can help us identify changing civilisations, even in the same region.

All forms of long-lasting pottery require the clay to be baked in an oven. If a vessel is made with only sun-dried clay, it cannot hold any liquid. But if it is heated (fired) in a kiln, to at least 500°C, irreversible chemical changes will occur within the clay to make the material stronger.

▲ *Aqueducts are ancient structures that carried water to fields and cities. Many of them required brick and clay*

🔍 The Appearance of Clay

Variations in the kiln and in firing give amazingly different kinds of pottery. Some ancient inventions in clay-based technologies include terracotta, ceramic, stoneware, porcelain, and china. Even in modern times, clay arts require much knowledge and skill, and the best clay pieces can be identified by region and artist. Clay was also used as an ingredient to make stronger building materials.

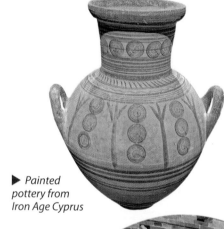

▶ *Painted pottery from Iron Age Cyprus*

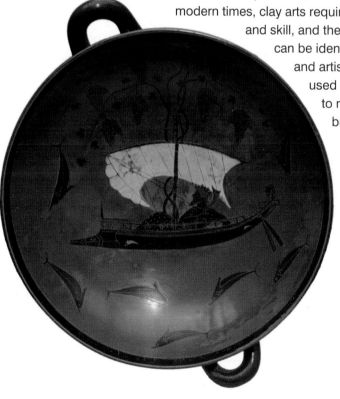

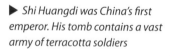

▶ *Shi Huangdi was China's first emperor. His tomb contains a vast army of terracotta soldiers*

◀ *The Greek god of grapes and wine, Dionysus, in a ship sailing among dolphins; black-figure pottery from Mycenaean Greece, c. 530 BCE*

Brick by Brick

The invention of bricks allowed humans to build the first cities. The earliest bricks were sun-dried blocks of clay mixed with things like straw and shale. In the Mesopotamian city of Ur—roughly modern-day Iraq—sun-baked bricks were used to build the first true arch. This happened during 4000 BCE. Eventually, people discovered the right mix of earthy ingredients to make the strongest bricks. They also fired bricks in kilns to make them more long-lasting.

In 210 BCE, engineers used both fired and sun-dried bricks to build the Great Wall of China. By 600 BCE, the Babylonians and Assyrians were adding a glaze or enamel to make coloured bricks. It is unfortunate that some of this ancient technology, the creation of certain blue glazes in particular, has been lost and cannot be recreated today.

▲ Brick ruins of a reservoir in Gujarat, India, which was part of the Indus Valley Civilisation

▼ Remains of an ancient Roman apartment block built with bricks

Cementing Success

Mortar is a slushy mix that is layered into the gaps between bricks or stones. It hardens in the air and holds the construction together more securely. Mortar is made of sand, water, and some kind of binder, such as lime. Ancient Egyptians developed the earliest known mortar in about 4,000 BCE. This was a soft paste of gypsum (plaster) and sand. The Romans used a slightly more advanced method to create lime mortars.

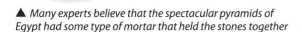

▲ Many experts believe that the spectacular pyramids of Egypt had some type of mortar that held the stones together

🔍 Roman Cement

About 2000 years ago, the ancient Greeks and Romans invented a type of cement that used lime and volcanic ash. These two compounds reacted in the presence of water to form a hard mass. The mix set very slowly and took centuries to harden completely. As a result, many Roman structures are still standing today, though they were built way back in the Iron Age. In comparison, some of our modern mortars used in bridges, roads, and buildings crumble in 50–100 years.

▲ In 79 CE, a volcanic eruption covered the ancient Roman city of Pompeii in lava. The cooling rock preserved the streets and buildings, including signs on shop fronts and Iron Age graffiti

🔍 Monument for the Ages

▲ The Basilica of Maxentius is a marvel of Roman engineering and would have been impossible without mortar

The word cement comes from the Latin word 'caementum', which referred to stone chips, like the ones used to make Roman mortar. It did not refer to the cement mixture itself. Most buildings in Rome made use of multiple materials to create comfortable homes and striking landmarks. For instance, the famous Pantheon of Rome was constructed in 123 CE using brick, but had an amazing dome of concrete that stretched across 43 m.

▲ Bathing was a social activity in Roman times. Ancient Roman baths were large constructions that required mortar

Glued Together

Our ancestors created glue from natural materials as far back as 200,000 BCE. Natural glues were used for ceremonies and decorations around 6000 years ago, and to fix axes and arrow tips about 5200 years back. Later, stronger glues were invented by boiling the bones, hides, and other parts of animals.

Animal Glue

Ancient Egyptians are thought to have first discovered the use of animal glue to make furniture. These were usually made only for royal and wealthy Egyptians who could afford them. As far back as 2500 years, the tombs of pharaohs were laden with laminated woodwork created by gluing the pieces together.

▲ *Pharaoh's chair in the Museum of Egyptian Antiques*

In Real Life

Collagen is a protein found in the skin and bones of animals. Amazingly, both glue and gelatine—from which jellies are made—were created by boiling collagen! Pure collagen mildly treated with acids or hot water gives gelatine. Less pure collagen, vigorously treated the same way, will produce sticky, dark animal glue.

Adhesives

Did you know the word adhesive can be used for any material that binds things together? This includes cement, glue, paste, mucilage, starch, and other substances you wouldn't normally call 'sticky'. About 3500 years ago, Egyptians were making papyrus, a writing surface, out of reed fibres glued together with flour paste.

◀ *This papyrus painting shows the pharaoh hunting a flock of birds as they rise above aquatic reeds*

Isn't It Amazing!

One square inch of modern super glue can hold around one ton. To give you some idea, a small car weighs about 1.5 tonnes.

The Many Uses of Glue

By Greek and Roman times, glue had become commonplace and was used for small jobs as well as for large building requirements. Chinese inventors at the time tried out adhesives made from fish, ox, and stag horns. They used glue not just for sticking things together but also to preserve paintings and for medical purposes.

▶ *Ancient Roman mosaics were made by gluing pieces of tiles in intricate patterns*

To Spin a Yarn

Clothes were first worn by proto humans called Neanderthals. They used animal hides to cover themselves and to show off their status! Then came the **Cro-Magnons**, who used needle-like tools to punch holes into hides and lace them up again.

▶ Prehistoric clothes of Otzi, the Iceman

Otzi the Iceman

Otzi the Iceman is a 5300-year-old human who showed us what prehistoric fashion was like. His clothes were made from the skins, bones, horns, and feathers of six types of animals. His attire also had leaves, wood, and fibre from 17 different trees.

A New Set of Threads

Felt is the name given to the first man-made cloth; that is, not leather or fur, but real fabric. Felt is made by matting, condensing, and pressing natural fibres together. It was invented well before spinning, weaving, and knitting.

The Sumerians believed that it was Urnamman of Lagash, who discovered the secret of felt-making. In time, many different techniques of felting were invented.

◀ A felt hat from the Loulan kingdom of Iron Age China

Weaving

The oldest bit of woven cloth dates to the 7th millennium BCE. It was used for wrapping the dead in Anatolia (present-day Turkey). Nalbinding, an early type of knitting, was seen soon after, around 6500 BCE.

In Japan, weaving was well established by 5500 BCE. Painted pottery from this time shows people wearing clothes. As civilisations discovered new fibres, they invented more ways of creating textiles.

In Real Life

Felt is still used today by nomadic people to create rugs, tents, and clothes. You have most likely seen felt in your arts and crafts classes.

▲ Kirghiz nomads shifting their felt home

Isn't It Amazing!

A 50,000-year-old needle is the oldest sewing tool in existence. But it is not like any sewing needle we see today. Instead, it is made from the bone of a large bird and has a bit of twine still attached to it.

▶ Denisova Cave in Siberia, Russia is a treasure trove of finds on early humans, including the world's oldest sewing needle

Discovery of Amazing Fibres

Linen was made by Egyptians around 4500 BCE. It was first used for bandaging mummies. Egyptians also tried out cloths made of rush, reed, palm, and papyrus; however, they considered animal fibres to be impure and taboo. Cotton was in use in ancient India by the 5th millennium BCE. Silk production began in China, probably around 5000–3000 BCE. Wool was used after sheep breeding took off in 3000 BCE.

| Egyptian Pharaoh | Egyptian Queen | Greek man | Greek woman | Roman man in a toga | Roman woman |

▲ *Ancient robes of different civilisations*

The Silk Road

This was a cross-continental east-west network that allowed merchants to exchange luxury goods. It brought great wealth to civilisations across China, India, Egypt, Central Asia, and Rome.

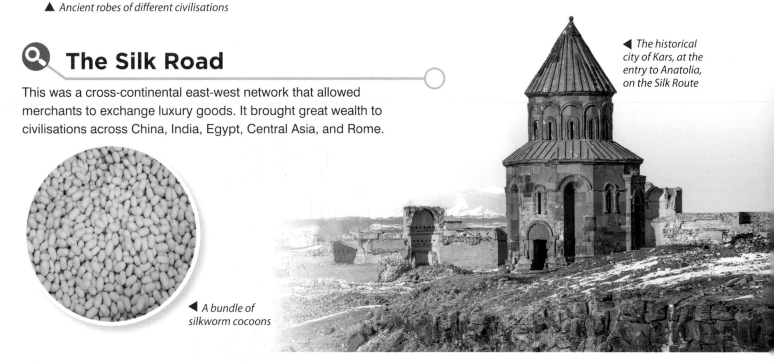

◀ *The historical city of Kars, at the entry to Anatolia, on the Silk Route*

◀ *A bundle of silkworm cocoons*

Loose Ends

Spinning is the word for pulling and twisting raw fibre into thread. Surprisingly though, spinning seems to have been invented after weaving. Around the time the Egyptians were producing linen, they invented the drop spindle, hand-to-hand spinning, and rolling the yarn on the thigh. They also knew of the horizontal ground loom and the vertical two-beam loom, both of which came from Asia.

▼ *The Egyptian drop spindle*

Fiercest Battle Inventions

Humans have fought each other since the dawn of our time on this planet. The earliest records of war however, date from 2700 BCE, when the Sumerian king Enmebaragesi fought and looted the **Elamite** people.

Over time, the need to wage successful wars brought amazing leaps in technology, science, and law. It also gave rise to awe-inspiring weapons that struck fear in the hearts of enemies.

▲ *An Assyrian charioteer and archer with shield bearers, possibly from an Iron Age battle against the Elamite city, Hamaru*

Spearheading the Charge

Originally a throwing weapon from Stone Age times, the spear evolved into different forms and functions. By 3000 BCE, Sumerian armies were charging in close-knit groups called phalanxes. They used the spear to thrust into the enemy at close range.

The Greeks refined the spear into a 2–3 m long weapon called the pike.

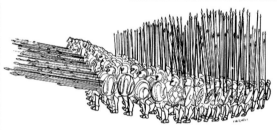

▲ *Philip II of Macedon developed the pike into the elongated sarissa, which was 4–6.5 m long. This gave his army of hoplites an offensive and defensive advantage*

◀ *Philip's son, Alexander the Great, used sarissa-bearing armies to conquer an empire*

▶ *The Romans used a long, heavy javelin called pilum. This was thrown by foot soldiers and cavalry*

◀ *This amphora from 540–530 BCE shows Greek champion Hercules wielding a pike and shield*

◀ *The phalanx became a standard formation of the Roman infantry*

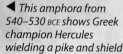

To Fire at Will

The bow and arrow are prehistoric inventions. It is said that they were made for hunting nearly 64,000 years ago in South Africa. Bows were originally made of springy woods and strung with animal gut. Around 1700 BCE, the composite bow was invented in various cultures of Asia. It was usually made of layers of wood, horns, and sinew glued together. By 1000 CE, horse-riding archers in central Asia had invented the recurved bow. It had a wide W shape that allowed even short bows to shoot far-off targets.

◀ *Diana, Greek goddess of the hunt, painted with a recurved bow in her hands*

▶ *This Turkish composite bow was clearly a cherished possession—it is decorated with pigments, gold, silver, and ivory*

🔍 Amazing Arrows

Arrows were made of wood and tipped with sharp flint, hard wood, horn, or metal. The oldest arrow points came from Africa some 64,000 years ago and were made of bone. In the 3rd century BCE, weapon-makers of India invented an all-metal arrow. They also might have made metal bows, but these became popular only in the 17th century CE.

▲ *Pharaoh Tutankhamen shooting at his enemies; section of a wooden painting done around 1327 BCE*

👤 In Real Life

The amazing *urumi*, meaning 'curling sword', is a flexible whip-like sword from prehistoric southern India. It might have been used in the northern Mauryan Dynasty near 350–150 BCE. It can be seen today in the martial arts of southern India: *Kalaripayattu* and *Silambam*.

▲ *It takes years to master the use of the urumi*

🔍 The Hero's Club

A lethal bludgeon from the Bronze Age, the mace is the first weapon invented specifically for war. It was fashioned out of rock and could smash body and bone. Naturally, such a hefty weapon was not for everyone; it was mostly used by champions and kings. By 3000 BCE, mace-heads were cast in elaborate shapes using copper at Mesopotamia, Syria, Palestine, and Egypt.

🔍 To Parry and Thrust

The sword became separate from the dagger during the Bronze Age. However, right up till Roman times, swords were still quite short and narrow. The technology for making true swords remained a mystery till medieval times.

▶ *A carving from 3100 BCE depicting Pharaoh Menes, the first ruler of a united Egypt. He is the earliest mace-bearing hero we know of by name*

▼ *A curved sword from Bronze Age Scandinavia*

Throw and Scatter

Not all weapons were for close-range use like the sword or the mace. There were many strong weapons invented for long-range combat like the crossbow or the catapult. Weapons like the caltrop were used in a clever manner to injure those on horseback.

🔍 Quick on the Trigger

The amazing repeating crossbow, the zhuge nu, was the first weapon to resemble modern automatic firing machines. The magazine atop the barrel held several pre-loaded arrows, which could be fired one after the other. This gave the soldier a deadly advantage over his opponent who fired more slowly, as he had to stop and reload an arrow after each shot.

So amazing was this invention, that it was seen in use during the war between China and Japan in 1894–1895. The development of the repeating crossbow is associated with Zhuge Liang, a brilliant military tactician of the Three Kingdoms period of China (220–280 CE). He developed a bow that could shoot many arrows at one time. Other accounts show that the repeating crossbow predates him.

▲ *The magazine and arrows of an ancient Chinese repeating crossbow*

🔍 Caltrops

Caltrops are small spiked weapons that are still used in modern warfare. Then, as now, they were scattered on the ground where they could fatally injure the enemies' horses and men. In 331 BCE, during the Battle of Gaugamela in modern Iraq, the Persians sowed the battlefield with caltrops to prevent Alexander the Great's troops from advancing. Although Alexander overcame them, he greatly admired the invention and adopted its use in later battles.

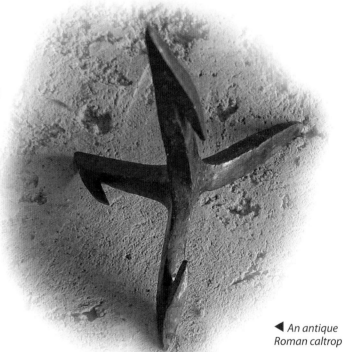

◀ *An antique Roman caltrop*

▲ *Caltrops were used in World War I to disable horses*

👤 In Real Life

Developed versions of the caltrops were used as weapons during World War II. The US, British, and French officers would parachute into enemy territory and release caltrops across their runways. The caltrops punctured the tires of all the vehicles that moved on the runway and sabotaged the enemy's operations.

Boomerang

Though associated with Aboriginal Australians, the boomerang was a popular hunting tool throughout Africa and Europe in ancient times. Not all boomerangs are designed to return when thrown. Some of them are fashioned like axes and used in combat between warriors. The oldest boomerang yet known was carved from the tusk of a mammoth and dates back to 23,000 BCE. It was found in a cave in Poland.

▲ Egyptian hunting boomerangs decorated with gold; treasures from Pharaoh Tutankhamun's tomb

▼ The Roman ballista was an ancient missile weapon that launched either bolts or stones at a distant target

◄ The heavy, naturally curved bone of mammoths' tusks could be used to make boomerangs

A Giant Catapult

Used to launch heavy objects such as rocks and large spears at far-off enemies, the ballista was invented by the Greeks. It was then refined by the Romans during the 3rd and 4th centuries BCE. The largest ballista of this time could accurately lob 27 kg weights to a distance of 450 m.

▼ Later modifications to the ballista turned it into an enormous machine that could fling flaming missiles into enemy armies and strongholds

Mightier than the Sword

Though speaking comes naturally to all of us, writing has to be formally learned. But when did writing systems evolve? In the 4th millennium BCE, trade and wealth were expanding rapidly. People needed a way to track their bargains, monies, properties, and other details. Kings also needed such information, so they could exact taxes for making roads and war. The first scripts were most likely invented as memory aids and bookkeeping tools. But they soon flourished to express larger, bolder, newer ideas that would change the world over and over again.

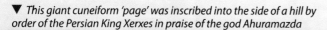
▼ This giant cuneiform 'page' was inscribed into the side of a hill by order of the Persian King Xerxes in praise of the god Ahuramazda

▶ Sumerian cuneiform is the earliest writing we know of. This cone from 1850 BCE records, 'Sin-kashid, mighty man, king of Uruk, king of the Amnanum, provider of the temple Eanna, built his royal palace'

▲ Ancient Egyptian scripts are called hieroglyphics, meaning 'sacred carvings'. You often see them on amazing murals accompanying gods and pharaohs

▼ Evidence of Chinese writing exists from 1500 BCE, but it likely developed well before that. This tortoise shell shows a divination from the time of King Wu Ding (1200 BCE)

▼ Hieroglyphic carvings at an ancient Egyptian temple

▼ One of the 12 clay tablets of the earliest known poem, 'The Epic of Gilgamesh', 2003–1595 BCE

Carved in Stone

The scripts of the 4th millennium BCE were etched on to clay tablets with a reed stylus. Sometimes, they were drawn with ink made of ground charcoal, powdered insects, plants, or natural pigments. People also wrote on bone, stone, wax tablets, animal skins, tanned leather, bark, and silk. Around 3100–2900 BCE, Egypt invented papyrus from reeds that grew by the River Nile. This was used in the form of washable, reusable scrolls, and to wrap mummies!

Around 104–105 CE, the imperial official Cai Lun showed his invention of paper to the Han emperor of China. It rapidly became the writing material of choice for the entire world.

▲ In ancient India, sacred and political texts would be recorded on strips of palm leaves tied together to form manuscripts

In Real Life

The invention of the alphabet powered most modern written languages. Most Western, Arabic, and Indian alphabets come from a system of writing popular in Syria in the 11th century BCE. The Greeks were the first to adapt it to their language, around 1000–900 BCE.

◀ The Code of Hammurabi is a stone tablet from 2nd millennium BCE recording the laws and punishments of its Babylonian king

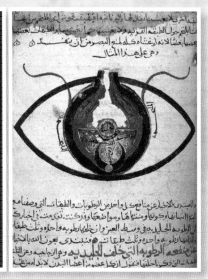

▲ Ancient alphabets: a Greek page from 'The Odyssey'; an Arabic medical page about the eye

▼ Some of the Dead Sea Scrolls (300 BCE– 200 CE), manuscripts of great importance to Christianity and Judaism, were written on thin, whitish leather

Which Way is North?

Did you know that Earth has two poles? What we think of as the top and bottom points of the planet are the geographic north and south poles, respectively. But, Earth also has magnetic north and south poles, which are hundreds of miles away from the true or geographic north and south. The compass, which is a magnetic device, will always point to the magnetic north pole. But when was it invented?

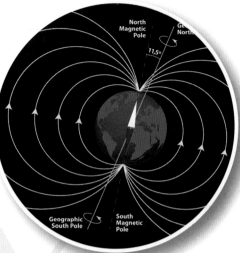

▶ Earth is a giant spinning magnet with moving magnetic poles and fixed geographic poles

⊛ Incredible Individuals

Chinese inventor Ma Jun (200–265 CE) built a chariot with a small statue atop that always pointed south. This clever contraption did not use magnets. It had a system of gears that turned the statue in the direction opposite to the chariot, but at the same angles. Thus, one could never be lost in a chaotic battlefield with such a tool.

Legend has it that the Qin dynasty (221–206 BCE) invented a south-pointing ship along similar lines. But it is more likely that the ship used magnets, which were well known to the Qin engineers.

🔍 Compass

Some scholars believe that the magnetic compass was invented by the Chinese during the 26th century BCE. Early magnetized needles were set on wood and floated in a basin of water. When the needle came to a standstill, its marked tip would point North-South. Records show a spoon-shaped compass dating from the ancient Han Dynasty. The magnetic spoon rested on a square bronze plate—representing Earth—that bore a circle—symbolizing heaven. The board was marked with constellations and astrological signs. The first Chinese emperor is said to have used such a divining board and compass in court to affirm his right to the throne! It would be several centuries more before the compass was put to practical use by travellers.

◀ Ma Jun's south-pointing chariot

💡 Isn't It Amazing!

If you had a compass 800,000 years ago, its needle would have pointed towards the southern hemisphere! Since its discovery in the early 19th century, the magnetic north has drifted over 966 km and continues to move every year. Scientists worry that the next pole swap could destroy our entire electric grid!

◀ This south-pointing spoon is a compass of the Chinese Han dynasty (202 BCE–220 CE)

A Gaze at Glass

Natural glass occurs when sand is hit by lightning or when molten lava cools rapidly. Humans used such glass, called obsidian, to make weapons, jewellery and money, long before they invented glass-making technologies. The Roman historian Pliny believed that glass was first made in 5000 BCE by Phoenician merchants around Syria. However, the earliest real evidence of man-made glass comes from 3500 BCE, from Egypt and Mesopotamia. People here were also the first to make glass vessels in 1500 BCE.

▲ *Ancient arrowhead made of obsidian*

▲ *Ancient Egyptian coffin mask made of dark glass and wood*

🔍 Recipe for Glass

We know how Mesopotamians made glass from ritual-like instructions they left behind on clay tablets. The ingredients include sand, soda ash, and 'white plant', which is an unknown substance. Some truly amazing colours were added by using metallic oxides.

Copper and cobalt compounds gave the glass royal blue and turquoise blue tints that are still popular today. The earliest glass-making manual belongs to the amazing library of Nineveh built by Ashurbanipal (669–631 BCE), the last great king of ancient Assyria.

▶ *Tinted glass vessels from ancient Rome*

🔍 Glass-blowing

Only the very rich and powerful could afford to buy glass in the early days. This changed when Syrians invented glass-blowing at the end of the 1st century CE. Suddenly, it was easier, faster, and cost-effective to make glass. For the first time, ordinary people could afford to buy and enjoy the convenience and beauty of glass products.

◀ *Ancient Syrian glass flask*

▶ *Miniature glassware from the 18th dynasty of ancient Egypt*

Creating Surplus

Historians often mark the beginning of civilisation as that crucial time when hunter-gatherers gave up wandering and began farming. Agricultural technologies allowed humans to literally reap the wealth of the earth. To farm successfully, we tamed rivers, mountains, and, of course, plants and animals. The farmers' labour and ingenuity created so much surplus that populations grew rapidly. With more people came specialised occupations and about 11,000 years of the most amazing advances in civilisation.

▲ The Fertile Crescent was a sickle-shaped land that was the birthplace of a number of technological innovations

◀ The first large network of dams and channels was created by Egypt's First Dynasty. It began in 3100 BCE under King Menes and led to the formation of Lake Moeris, which is still around

▲ The Egyptians invented the Nilometer in the 3rd century BCE. It is a measuring column sunk into the river to check flood levels

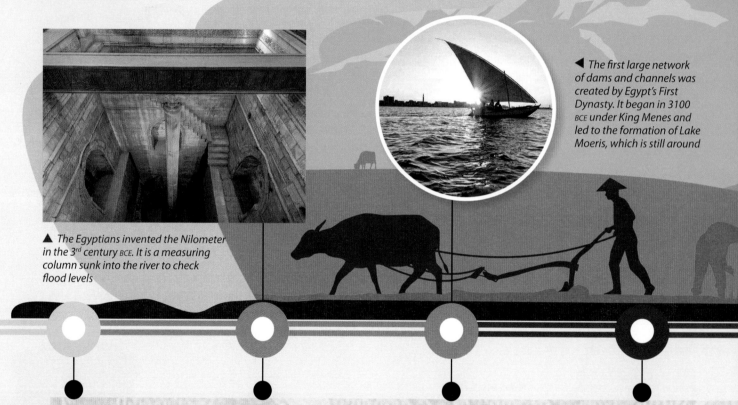

9500 BCE
The eight founding crops of agriculture—emmer and einkorn wheat, barley, peas, lentils, bitter vetch, chickpeas, and flax—are cultivated in the Fertile Crescent.

8000 BCE
Agriculture begins in parts of the Americas as hunter-gatherers grow wild crops to broaden their food sources. Squash is one of these early crops.

6000 BCE
Irrigation begins: the floodwaters of the Nile (in Egypt) and the rivers Tigris and Euphrates (in Mesopotamia) are diverted to the fields over July–December and then drained back into the rivers.

2800 BCE
The first evidence of a ploughed field is seen at Kalibangan. The area was part of the Indus Valley Civilisation.

▲ *Three water wheels in front of the Azem Palace, Syria*

👥 In Real Life

The fertile Indian subcontinent was ideal for ancient farmers. Oranges, wheat, and legumes were easily cultivated. Dates and mangoes appeared by 4,000 BCE. By 2,000 BCE, teas, bananas, rice, and apples were being grown. Over the next millennium, coconuts were being exported to Africa and eggplants were in cultivation.

▶ *Modern rice farms in mountainous China*

◀ *The counter-weighted Shadoof raising water up from a low river with steep banks*

1700 BCE

When the river is not in flood, an invention called the Shadoof allows farmers to lift water for irrigating fields using a bucket. By 700 BCE, this is further eased by the invention of the water wheel, which required little human effort.

500 BCE

Greece uses crop rotation methods on large estates.

▶ *A hydraulic-powered trip hammer*

100 BCE

The Chinese invent the hydraulic-powered trip hammer to pound and polish grain.

100 CE

The Chinese invent the square-pallet chain pump. It is powered by a water-wheel or pulled by oxen. It raises water up into channels that irrigate farmland on high ground.

Preserving Food

While hunter-gatherers ate a variety of vegetables and meats depending on the season and their location, the farmers continued to eat the limited crops they planted. Farmers also suffered due to floods, droughts, and pest attacks, all of which could leave them starving. The need to overcome hunger and find variety in food led early man to invent numerous ways of cooking and storing foods.

The Art of Preserving Food

Early humans found varied ways to extend the shelf life of food. These included heating raw food, drying and smoking to remove water, pickling, fermentation, etc. Such measures served the twin benefits of preventing bacteria and yeast from spoiling food, while also introducing the early man to a variety of flavours and textures.

⊛ Incredible Individuals

It is said that Queen Cleopatra of Egypt ate pickles as part of her beauty diet. Julius Caesar fed pickles to his armies. He believed it gave them spiritual and physical strength. While that might have been just a belief, their army certainly conquered several kingdoms!

▲ *Pickling was known to the Mesopotamians as early as 2400 BCE*

The Oldest Form of Cooking

In its earliest form, baking was done by dry-roasting grains or cooking a batter of water and cereals over fire. The Egyptians may have been the first to use the oven for baking. By c. 2600 BCE, they were also using **leavening**—the raising agent in bread.

▶ *Funerary model of a bakery and brewery, from ancient Egypt's 11th dynasty*

◀ *A Syrian baking mould from 2nd millennium BCE shows goats and a cow being attacked by a lion*

A Fishy History

Fishing nets, spears, lines, and rods appeared in Egypt around 3500 BCE. In Greece and Rome, surplus fish were stored in a fermented form called 'garum', a popular condiment.

A Pinch of Salt

First discovered around 6050 BCE, salt was a valuable trade commodity. In China, peasant families would set aside a jar of salted vegetables every year. These were given to the daughter upon her marriage. The Chinese used salt not directly, but through condiments like soy sauce and fish paste. The Egyptians even used salt for funeral offerings. They mixed brine, that is, saltwater, with vinegar to form a sauce called 'oxalme', which was later used by the Romans.

▲ The ancient Chinese way of boiling brine to produce salt

A Dash of Sugar

The grass called sugar cane was refined into sugar c. 500 BCE in India. By c. 200 BCE, the crop was being grown in China. In c. 510 BCE, soldiers of the Persian king Darius found 'reeds which produce honey without bees' near the Indus River. Sugar, like salt, is an excellent preservative. However, it also attracts moisture. Sugar water causes microorganisms to begin the fermentation process, which produces alcohol. It is likely that some form of the drink was discovered this way!

◄ Sugar cane helps in 80 per cent of the world's sugar production

In Real Life

In ancient Rome, salt was so valuable, it could be used in place of money. In fact, many Roman workers and soldiers were paid in salt. In Latin, the word salarium meant a payment made in salt. It gives us the modern word, salary.

▶ Bolivia's Salar de Uyuni is the world's largest and highest salt flat. It is the remnant of a prehistoric lake

Isn't It Amazing!

The Chinese discovered fermentation and distillation 9,000 years ago. They were probably the first people to drink alcohol.

Word Check

Alloys: In the making of metals, alloys are formed by mixing two or more pure metals. This creates new types of metals that are suitable for different technologies.

Assyria: It is a historical region and civilisation, not to be confused with Syria! At its peak, Assyria stretched from northern Mesopotamia through modern Turkey and down to Egypt.

Bipedal: Using two legs for walking

c.: This is an abbreviation for the word 'circa', which means about or approximately.

Cro-Magnon: It is an erect and tall race of ancient humans of France. They were among the earliest *Homo sapiens* on Earth.

Elamite: the people of Elam, an ancient kingdom. It lay next to Sumer and stretched north from the coast of the Persian Gulf.

Fossils: The remains of a prehistoric plant or animal buried under a rock is known as a fossil. Fossils are studied to discover more about the time period to which they belong.

Hoplite: It refers to an armed foot-soldier from ancient Greece.

Leavening: It is a substance that, when mixed into a dough and baked, gives you light, fluffy foods, such as bread and cake. Modern-day leavening agents include yeast and baking powder.

Macedon: It was an ancient country in northern Greece. It was home to Alexander the Great.

Mesopotamia: It is a Greek word for 'two rivers'. This name refers to the historical area between the rivers Tigris and Euphrates. It was dominated by the Sumerian, Akkadian, Assyrian, and Babylonian civilisations.

Proto humans: They are also called archaic humans. This phrase describes closely-related human species that lived on earth thousands of years ago. This includes *Homo neanderthalensis* (Neanderthals) and *Australopithecus afarensis*. All of them are now extinct, except for *Homo sapiens*, the modern humans.

Reservoir: A man-made lake. It usually stores flood or rainwater for use during the dry season.

Scribes: Few people in ancient times knew how to read and write. Official writing and record-keeping jobs were therefore given to scholarly people called scribes.

Tutankhamun: He is possibly the most famous Pharaoh since 1922, when British archaeologist Howard Carter unearthed his treasure-filled tomb in Egypt's Valley of the Kings.